I0762673

First Phrases from Around the World
Everyday German
Kim Thompson
Little Mitchie
an imprint of Mitchell Lane

Creating Young Nonfiction Readers

Little Mitchie lets children delve into nonfiction at beginning reading levels. Young readers are introduced to new concepts, facts, ideas, and vocabulary.

Tips for Reading Nonfiction with Young Readers

Talk about Nonfiction

Begin by explaining that nonfiction books give us information that is true. The book will be organized around a specific topic or idea, and we may learn new facts through reading.

Look at the Parts

Most nonfiction books have helpful features. Our *Little Mitchie* titles include color photographs and graphic aids, a table of contents, and an index. Share the purpose of these features with your reader.

Color Photos and Graphic Aids

A lot of information can be found by "reading" photos, charts, maps, and other graphic aids found within nonfiction texts. Help your reader learn more about the different ways information can be displayed.

Table of Contents

Located at the front of the book, this list shows the big ideas within the text and the page numbers where they can be found.

Index

Located at the back of the book, an index is an alphabetical list of topics and the page numbers where they can be found.

With a little help and guidance about reading nonfiction, you can feel good about introducing a young reader to the world of *Little Mitchie* nonfiction books.

Mitchell Lane
PUBLISHERS

2001 SW 31st Avenue
Hallandale, FL 33009
www.mitchelllanepub.com

Copyright © 2026 by Mitchell Lane Publishers. All rights reserved. No part of this book may be reproduced without written permission from the publisher. Printed and bound in the United States of America.

First Edition, 2026.

Author: Kim Thompson
Designer: Kathy Walsh
Editor: Tricia Hoffman

Names/credits: Kim Thompson
Title: First Phrases from Around the World
Everyday German
Description: Hallandale, FL:
Mitchell Lane Publishers, [2026]

Series: First Phrases from Around the World
Library bound ISBN: 979-8-89260-541-0
Paperback ISBN: 979-8-89260-583-0
ebook ISBN: 979-8-89260-549-6

Little Mitchie is an imprint of
Mitchell Lane Publishers

PHOTO CREDITS
Cover and Title pg: Adobe Stock: iukhym_vova, smile3377; Doodle Art Adobe: devitaayu, FourLeafLover, wanchana, veekicl, Rizky, mhatzapa, Kebon doodle, Asyam Design, piixypeach, syoko: istock: background, rica nohara; p4, Emely; p5, romrodinka, riza1999; p6, djedzura; p 10 visualspace, SolStock; p13, Bet_Noire, FatCamera; p14, yacobchuk: Shutterstock: p4, Andrew Angelov, Irina Wilhauk; p6, Roman Samborskyi; p7, Yuliya Evstratenko, Oksana Shufrych, Eric Isselee; p9, waldru, p12, Chiociolla, BongoStock, Saleman; p15, Gorodenkoff; p16, BearFotos, Prostock-studio, marino bocelli; p17, JoeSAPhotos; p18, Prostock-studio, Gorodenkoff, Sana Grebinets; p19, michaeljung; p20, Elipetit, Ground Picture, Donna Ellen Coleman, Andrii Lemelianenko; p21, BarthFotografie, Avocado_studio, New Africa, Chase D'animulls, GSDesign; p22, Ground Picture, New Africa; p23, Evgeny Atamanenko, Kidsada Manchinda: Alamy: p10, Soumen Hazra; p11, RooM the Agency; p12, Chris Brigne, Tetra Images LLC; p14, True Images, p14, 15, 19, 21, Cavan Images; p22, Alcibbum Photography/Fadil Aziz

Table of Contents

This Is Me

Ich bin neun Jahre alt.

I am nine years old.

Mein Name ist Elke.

My name is Elke.

Das ist ich

eins
one
zwei
two
drei
three
vier
four
fünf
five
sechs
six
sieben
seven
acht
eight
neun
nine
zehn
ten
Auf Wiedersehen!
Goodbye!

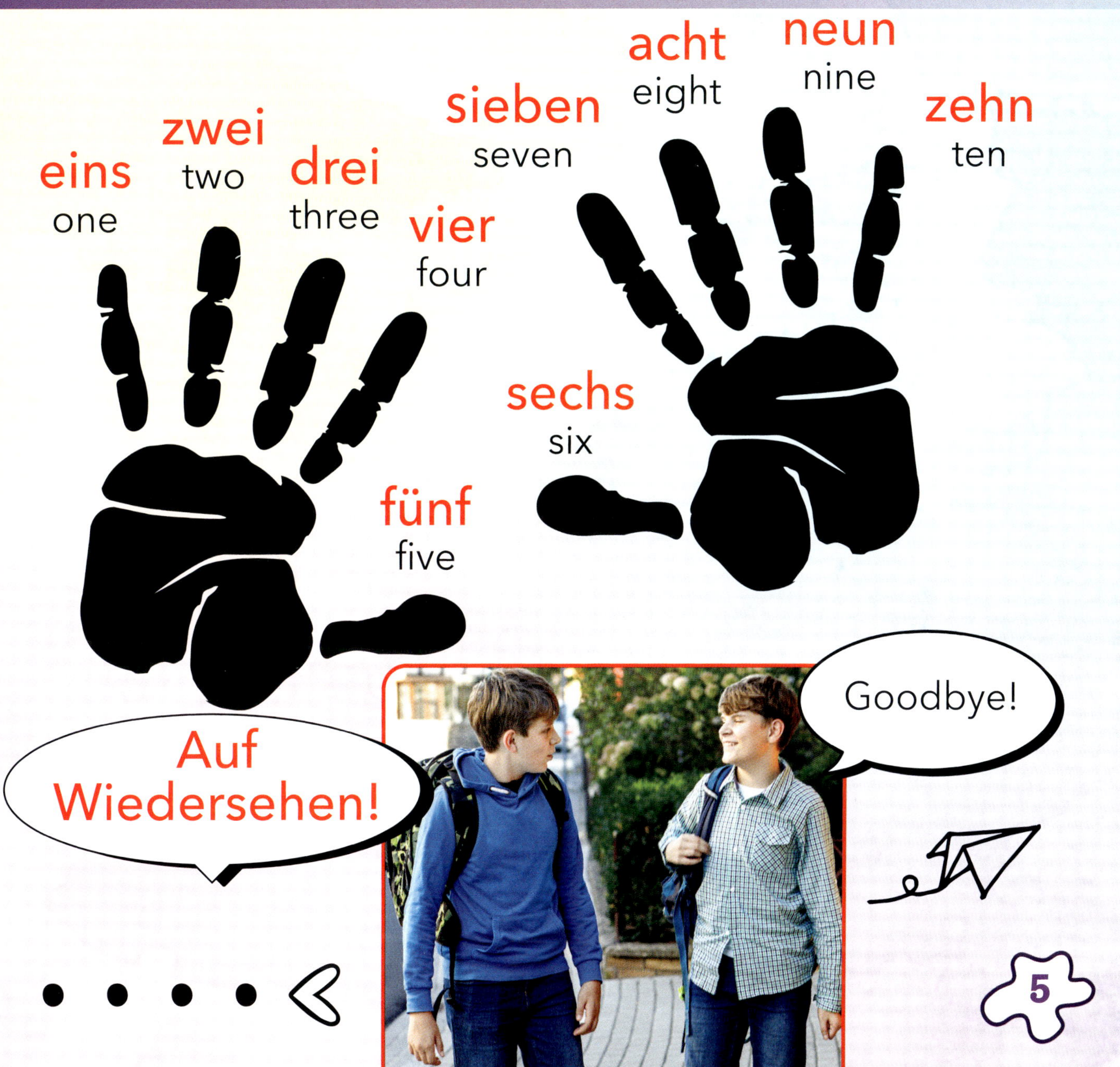

People and Pets

Menschen und Haustiere

Today

Heute ist Montag.

Today is Monday.

Sonntag
Sunday

Montag
Monday

Dienstag
Tuesday

Mittwoch
Wednesday

Donnerstag
Thursday

Freitag
Friday

Samstag
Saturday

Der Monat ist November.

The month is November.

Januar	January
Februar	February
März.	March
April.	April
Mai.	May
Juni	June
Juli	July
August.	August
September . . .	September
Oktober	October
November . . .	November
Dezember. . . .	December

Heute

Draußen ist es kalt.
It is cold outside.
heiß
hot
sonnig
sunny
regnerisch
rainy
windig
windy

Morning

Ich kämme meine Haare.

I comb my hair.

Ich putze mir die Zähne.

I brush my teeth.

Morgen

Ich trage einen gelben Hut.

I wear a yellow hat.

orange	gelb	blau	grün
orange	yellow	blue	green

rot	rosa	lila	schwarz	weiß
red	pink	purple	black	white

Breakfast

Ich möchte bitte Müsli zum Frühstück.

I want cereal for breakfast, please.

Brot
bread

Orangensaft
orange juice

Milch
milk

Ei
egg

Der Bus ist da.
Es ist Zeit zu gehen!

The bus is here.
It is time to go!

Schulbus
school bus

Rucksack
backpack

School

Ich lese.

I read.

Ich mache Mathe.

I do math.

Schule

Ich brauche Hilfe.

I need help.

Schreibtisch
desk

Lehrerin
teacher

Darf ich auf die Toilette gehen?

May I go to the bathroom?

Time to Play

Wirst du mit mir spielen?
Will you play with me?
Ja!
Yes!
Ich laufe.
I run.
Ich schwinge.
I swing.

Zeit zum Spielen

Neighborhood

Ich lebe in einer Nachbarschaft.

I live in a neighborhood.

Ich winke meinem Freund zu.

I wave to my friend.

Ich gehe in den Laden.

I go to the store.

Nachbarschaft

Wie viel kostet das?
How much does this cost?

Haus
house

Einfahrt
driveway

Straße
street

Roller
scooter

Dinner

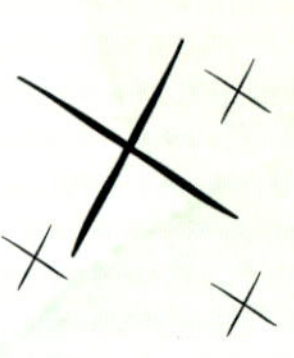

Ja, bitte.
Yes, please.

Nein, danke.
No, thank you.

Entschuldigen Sie.
Excuse me.

Abendessen

Ich mag deutsches Essen.
I like German food.

Schnitzel
schnitzel

Spätzle
spaetzle

Bratwurst
bratwurst

Stollen
stollen

Kartoffelchips
potato chips

Ich mag amerikanisches Essen.
I like American food.

Hotdog
hot dog

Night

Ich trage Pyjamas.

I wear pajamas.

Ich gehe ins Bett.

I go to bed.

Ich schließe meine Augen.

I close my eyes.

Nacht

Gute Nacht!
Kissen
pillow
Good night!
Decke
blanket
Teddybär
teddy bear

Index

About German

Approximately 130 million people speak German either as a first language or second language. It is the twelfth most common language in the world. German is the official language of six countries, all in Europe: Austria, Belgium, Germany, Liechtenstein, Luxembourg, and Switzerland. There are many dialects of German spoken in Germany and in the surrounding regions. High German dialects tend to be used in areas of Germany with hills and mountains. Low German dialects tend to be used in flatter areas. One unique thing about German is that almost all nouns always begin with a capital letter.